In the Fish Tank

Written by Alison Milford

RISING STARS

The children look at the fish in the fish tank.

They can see an eel. Can you see it too?

This tank has lots of bright fish from the reef.

Look! A shoal of fish is zipping across the tank.

The tang fish is flat.

The sweetlips fish has spots.

The parrot fish has big teeth.

The broomtail fish has long fins.

In the rock pool you might see ...

limpet shells

a crab

weed

Ask an adult if you can pick up a crab.

The fish in this deep tank are looking for food.

Big fish can look a bit odd!

moonfish

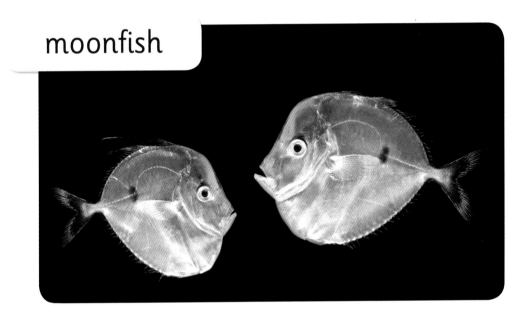

toadfish

Talk about the book

Ask your child these questions:

1 Why shouldn't you bang on the glass?

2 What was inside the first tank in the book?

3 Which fish had spots?

4 Which fish had big teeth?

5 Why should you ask an adult if you can pick up a crab?

6 What would you like to see at an aquarium?